9 STEPS TO SUCCESSFULLY NAVIGATE CORPORATE CULTURE

INTERPERSONAL ECONOMICS

LEARN TO BUILD RELATIONSHIPS AND ADVANCE YOUR CAREER

PAUL E. BRYANT

Wasteland Press
www.wastelandpress.net
Shelbyville, KY USA

Interpersonal Economics:
9 Steps to Successfully Navigate Corporate Culture
by Paul E. Bryant

First Printing – February 2014
Paperback ISBN: 978-1-60047-935-9
Hardback ISBN: 978-1-60047-936-6

Printed in the U.S.A.

0 1 2 3 4 5 6 7 8 9

ACKNOWLEDGEMENTS

My former students - at the Wesley House, C4k, Upward Bound, Impact One, Douglas County Correction Center, Buffett Middle School, Franklin and Belvedere Elementary Schools and the University of Nebraska at Omaha. *I am honored with the privilege to have taught you...*

Robin, Mom, Bob, Janice, Brazier, Paul II, Madison, Travis, Thel - *Family is everything. You are my world. I thank God for your support and critique.*

Mark, Tony, Doug, Larry, Barry, B.J., Ethel, Rhonda, Kevin, Cortney, Koang, Cheryl, Mark L, Willey – *Iron sharpens iron; Interacting with you inspired much of this work.*

John, Dean, Peter, Tony, Virgil, Dan, Shawn, Wally, Dick – *I am able to stand tall because you have decided to support my efforts... God bless you!*

Martin, Lynnell, Selwin, Maurice, Barlowe, Dick – *You lead and I'll follow...*

Faye & Clyde, Mark & Melanie, Joel & Felicia, Rob & Tina, Lawrence & Vickie, Kaynett & Guss Coach, Gooch, Badgett, – *You inspire me... Friends, how many of us have them?*

Allan, Gale, Stedman, George – *You challenge me to become my best self.*

1st National Bank, the Gallup Organization, Wells Fargo, Urban League, International Association of Chiefs of Police and the United Methodist Community Center, Inc. – *Thank you for all the experience!*

This book was written with my hands and edited with many of your eyes... (No ghost writers or professional editors; we did it!) I pray it achieves the desired results...

Every student who contributed to the research – *Thank you for your intellect.*

Stephen A. – You are the first person to say after an introduction, *"I've read your book!" Humbled...*

My mission in life is to teach people to look inside themselves to find their God given talents, and then inspire them to utilize their gifts toward the betterment of mankind.

I dedicate this book to anyone seeking advancement, may it be the key that unlocks their dormant human potential.

Paul E. Bryant

Learn more about the Author at the end of the book!

TABLE OF CONTENTS

PREFACE

Library shelves are crammed with self-help literature. You can find everything from how to eat better, think better, parent better and love better. You name it and there's been a book written to tell you how to do it better. The only reason to purchase one of these books is to learn something to improve a specific area of your life. Unfortunately many of these books are nothing more than compilations of clever sounding antidotes. Reasonable people will ask the following questions before purchasing any 'how-to' guide':

1. *Do the concepts actually work and*
2. *Will they work for me?*

The obvious next questions for you should be; *"What about this book? Will it deliver? Can it help me establish better workplace relationships?"*

I can tell you unequivocally 'YES'! Every principle discussed in these chapters is guaranteed to help you advance your career. These are the jewels retained from my diverse twenty-five year career. This manuscript is more than regurgitated quantitative, qualitative or regression analysis. It is a collection of the select nuggets of wisdom I learned from the University of Life. Enclosed are the experiences I learned firsthand as:

- The CEO of three distinct nonprofit agencies
- An Officer for the nation's largest independently owned bank
- A Business Banker for the nation's fourth largest bank
- A Senior Vice President for an International Corporation
- A University Professor

I've learned that you never get a second chance to make a first impression and this book is guaranteed to teach you how to make the most positive, memorable, impression possible.

My story is similar to others striving to make it out of the inner city. I've been run over by a car, survived a life threatening illness, witnessed my father's fatal shooting; dealt drugs, etc., etc. Poet, Langston Hughes said it best, *"Life for me ain't been no crystal stair."* My career was not the result of a long term strategic plan. I've been blessed…

By the grace of God, I received favor. While in the presence of persons in authority, I kept quiet, listened and learned. Their presence seemed to illuminate the pathway to success. I learned principals and applied practices that enabled me to maneuver in any environment. I was able to gain acceptance from those high in society to those least in notoriety; I went from kickin-it in the streets to private parties in corporate suites. From the back streets to the boardrooms, the tools in this book empowered me to succeed anywhere.

My older brother and I were the first in our family to earn college degrees, however our entrance into the job market was totally different. My brother was studious and took advantage of his education. After graduation he landed a great position with a Fortune 500 Company. When I graduated the only thing I received was a stack of rejection letters! I didn't receive one job offer.

Why??? Quite honestly, I didn't maximize my undergraduate opportunities. The epitome of the student athlete who was 90% athlete and 10% student; I felt the world owed me something. College was my ticket to play professional football. School was only a stepping stone to the NFL. I was a three year starter on a full scholarship. I reveled in the notoriety and good times. However, an injury my senior year erased the dream and without a Plan B, I spiraled into the abyss.

I remained in school while enduring a two-year pity party. I was deflated, depressed, and demoralized and did some really dumb things like dealing drugs. Thank God, I never got caught… I didn't focus in class and only did enough to get by. I kept my private life secret and somehow managed to graduate. Even though my family was proud of the accomplishment, the cold reception from the job market was a direct reflection of my lack of preparation. Every rejection letter was affirmation I was not ready for a professional job.

So there I stood, a college graduate, the pride of my family, without a job and no promising prospects. As strange as it sounds, my best option was to enroll in graduate school. Blessed with a second chance, I decided to get it right the second time around. Dedication, hard work and doing the right thing paid off. I stopped dealing and eventually earned two Masters Degrees! My next foray into the job market was much more successful.

The revelation I received upon entering the hallowed halls of corporate America was unmistakable; school had prepared me to enter the business world, but progressing would require a totally different set of skills. Fortunately, I learned from my mistakes and through osmosis developed tools to advance my career. Over the years I've shared these discoveries with university students, professional athletes, prisoners and senior executives; all have been enriched...

If you are interested in techniques that will position you for success, read this book. You will collect a few arrows for your corporate quiver. They worked for me and I guarantee they will work for you… (or mail your book to me for a full refund.)

Learn more about the Author at the end of the book!

INTERPERSONAL ECONOMICS

Standard economics records after-the-fact transactions; for example: *how many text messages does one send per day?* Behavioral economics is the science of choice; what people are thinking before they make transactions; *why do they send text messages?* Interpersonal economics assesses the power of ones influence to sway transactions; *when one sends text messages, how quickly does the receiver read and respond to them*? It's the emotional involvement or commitment between people.

Your perceptions create your reality. Multiple positive interactions with someone will establish a high degree of trust. Most people however are not aware of their influence on the perceptions of others. They fail to make the connection between their initial actions and first impressions. This oversight provides immeasurable opportunities within the market place.

Historically there has been an inability to measure interpersonal occurrences. Traditional economic concepts lack the metrics to understand interpersonal events or account for personalized interactions. It is difficult to measure motivation, communication styles, verbal and nonverbal message systems, problem solving, decision making and intuition.

If you step back and look at it, the Economic life cycle in a company is a series of communication happenstances; executives to managers, managers to workers, workers to clients, workers among themselves. Each of these interactions has considerable impact on the bottom line of the business but is overlooked by the standard economic theory.

What would happen in the following hypothetical situation? On Monday morning, the CEO of a company tells his executive management team they will lay off 35% of the workforce at the end of the week. His reasoning is that the workforce is lazy and incompetent. In reality, the company has fallen behind market trends and its products are dated. This problem is well known and has been murmured throughout the company for a couple of years. However, leadership has failed to address it.

At 11:00am, one of the executives leaks his explanation to a front line manager who in turn tells several workers. By 1:00pm, the president's words have gone viral and now every employee in the company from the CFO to the custodian knows how the president feels about the workforce.

How do you think those front line employees will respond? It's very doubtful customers of that company will experience exceptional customer service that week. Most employees will be more concerned about their livelihoods rather than the needs of customers. After the smoke has cleared from the layoffs, how will that CEO explain a decline in sales? There is no metric for low employee morale.

In a paper titled, The Economics of Interpersonal Relationships, Shemlah Naphish makes an interesting comparison between building relationships and money.

"The interactions of human relationships are like economic transactions similar to deposits and withdrawals at the bank. People unconsciously take mental notes of the good you do, and when you do good for someone it's like depositing money in your bank account.

Over time, as you develop a deeper relationship, you essentially acquire more money in this symbolic bank. Then when you need a favor or anything of that sort, you have the ability to make a withdrawal, and it will be ok and potentially reciprocated.

If you continually deposit more than the other person the relationship may become imbalanced and one-sided. Eventually this type of relationship ends in turmoil and causes emotional damage."

Interpersonal Economics is for those looking to establish positive relationships. Mastery of

Interpersonal communications will increase ones sense of well-being and advance their career. The art of influence in personal and consumer interactions will enable users to make wise choices and develop trust. Trust is the foundation for any relationship; personal or business. It's an advantage to know the wants and likes of others. People make decisions based off emotions and need to feel circumstances are right before they will give their trust.

During a job interview, how beneficial would it be for you to know the top-of-mind issues facing the person you were interviewing with, or how useful would it be to know the personal habits of someone you were trying to sell something to? In this book you will learn tools to build relationships which provide unlimited opportunities. Interpersonal trust emerges through unplanned civility; this trust is a determining factor in the economic decision making process. People like doing business with those with whom they like. Everything is easier when you do it with a friend.

Many companies don't understand positive employee/customer relations increases Interpersonal trust which will improve bottom line economic performance. When customers think you understand their needs, you become a trusted partner and advisor. Relationships will always undermine price; how often do you patronize a particular business because you have a "friend" that works there? People travel farther and spend more money in establishments that make them feel special.

Dismissing the value of Interpersonal trust can produce detrimental effects for an organization. It's not only bad for customers; it impacts the workforce. Bad employee relations lowers morale and low morale decreases employee satisfaction. High levels of employee dissatisfaction will increase turnover and increases in turnover equate to an inexperienced workforce. An inexperienced workforce will result in an overreliance on veteran employees. This may cause the most valuable assets in the organization to become disengaged. The combination of all these factors does not create an environment that is welcoming to customers. The quality of workplace relationships influences employee satisfaction and economic performance.

Interpersonal Economics not only helps a business grow its base of loyal customers; it helps that company retain its employees. Smart employers know positive relationships throughout the organization influences employee well-being; they place high value on workplace relationships. In certain sectors relationships are more important than wages in determining employee satisfaction and well-being.

BE WISE…

There was a time when people attended college to simply live more meaningful lives, but today people pursue higher education because a degree has become a mandatory workforce requirement. A national survey conducted by the Gallup Poll revealed the number #1 reason Americans attend college is to "Get a good job." According to Gallup CEO Jim Clifton, a good job is now the great global dream. He recently authored a book titled, *The Coming Jobs War*. During an interview with Forbes magazine he said, *"A good job is the number one social value for everyone. 'A good job' is more important than having a family, more compelling than democracy and freedom, religion and peace. Those are all very important but they are now subordinate to the almighty good job. This is one of our most powerful findings ever!"*

I agree with his assessment, I always viewed a good job as the gateway to a better life and a college degree as the prerequisite for getting a good job. My brother and I graduated from different colleges during the same week. We officially changed the legacy for future generations of our family; a college degree would no longer be a wish, it was now an expectation. It was a proud moment for our family when we walked across those stages. Our tickets to great jobs and prosperous futures had been officially punched.

My brother landed a great job. Unfortunately for me, my undergraduate degree didn't pay any dividends. Along the way many mentors had shared insights concerning what it takes to become successful. I'm sure every student has heard some version of this maxim – *Go to class, work hard, get a good education and once you graduate, you will get a good job.* My receptivity to that message depended on the level of success achieved by the person giving it.

I'll admit it; as an undergraduate student, my focus wasn't clear. A four year football scholarship, visions of playing in the NFL, unlimited freedom, girls... There were numerous options vying for my attention and studying didn't often win. My work ethic was sketchy and my lack of success in the job market was a direct reflection of that mediocre effort.

Nothing will soften a hard head like failure; so when I entered graduate school I decided to heed their counsel. "*Go to class, work hard, get a good education and once you graduate, you will get a good job,*" Maybe, just maybe; good grades were what it takes to become successful. I followed their advice and went to class, worked hard, and eventually earned two Masters Degrees!

I remember receiving the acceptance letter from my first employer as clearly as if it happened yesterday. It was like music to my ears to read those eight words every job applicant wants to hear; "*We would like to extend you an offer."* I was hired to join the management training program for one of the premier financial institutions in the country.

I felt totally prepared to ingratiate the workforce with skills and abilities refined through education. With all the competitiveness of an ex-athlete, I was ready to climb the corporate ladder of success as quickly as possible.

However, after my first day on the job I realized there were lessons about the workplace for which I was totally unaware.

The new trainee class was to meet for orientation at 8:00am. I walked through the door at 8 o'clock sharp, anxious to begin my ascent up the corporate ladder.

To my surprise, the other trainees were already in the room with orientation packets in their hands. The coordinator was giving instructions when I entered. Once I stepped in she said, *"Oh here he is..."* She held out a packet, turned to the other trainees and said, *"OK, let's begin the tour."*

She seemed annoyed and didn't bother to introduce herself or ask my name. I could tell by the conversations between other trainees that they had already been introduced. I tried to interject myself in a couple of conversations but didn't perceive my attempts were warmly received, so I quit trying. My classmates continued to bond during the morning coffee break while I sat alone and drank a solitary cup of coffee. I questioned, "*Was I late*?" "*Was this normal behavior or was I just overwhelmed by the first day?*" I rationalized, "*I am a leader; an eagle and eagles don't flock. They fly higher and see farther than other birds. They weren't talking to me because they could sense I was a high achiever; they were intimidated by my presence.*" This was natural selection; I was solo because I was positioned for success.

At noon the other trainees departed for lunch and I sat alone in the office pondering where to eat. They made plans for lunch and no one invited me! It was clear, I wasn't an eagle; I was the odd man out. I had gone half the day without anyone engaging me in a conversation. A number of questions ran through my mind as I rationalized my status as the invisible man. "*Was I receiving this treatment because I didn't major in finance or because I was black? Or... was it possibly the brown suit?*" Twenty five years of corporate experience has now taught me it was a combination of things; my timing, my attitude and yes… the brown suit!

At the time I had no idea how significant a suit could be. People begin to gauge your status, character, and ability based on how you look. A man's suit is the single most important garment he will wear in corporate America. It helps establish his position as superior, equal, or inferior. Dark blue and gray suits lend the most credibility in business. The darker the suit, the more authority it transmits.

The statement my light brown suit made was, *"He is not powerful and He has no authority."* This was my introduction to the power of a positive first impression.

Thank God this 'less than stellar start' was not the end of my career. After learning the ropes and utilizing the techniques introduced in this book, I went on to enjoy an extremely successful professional career. I was promoted to an Officer in that bank and managed a $50 million loan program. Later in my career I managed a $75 million loan portfolio for another bank and served as a Senior Vice President and division manager for The Gallup Organization. I was the CEO of three different non-profit agencies; the Urban League of Nebraska, the United Minority Contractors Association and the United Methodist Community Center Inc. I've also taught courses at three different Universities and written three books of which the first was nominated for a Pulitzer Prize. My ascension up the corporate ladder was successful because I learned and then cloned the traits of successful leaders. I studied them closely, discovered what worked for them, and then added my flavor to it. The final result was a crisp, upwardly mobile, corporate persona that took me from the back streets to the board rooms.

I did an exceptional job climbing the corporate ladder which led to ample opportunities to observe corporate culture from a bird's eye view. I noticed certain traits exhibited by individuals in managerial positions, an unwritten code for executive behavior. They had similar mannerisms that weren't taught but were essential to becoming a member of the club. If you didn't have them, you wouldn't fit in.

I also noticed missteps repeatedly made by entry level employees looking to climb the ladder. It didn't matter what position they held or the organization, they always seemed to make the same mistakes. Like a young Paul Bryant sporting a light brown suit on his first day of work, they were unknowingly stepping on land mines they didn't know existed.

A Gallup Poll says 50% of Americans don't think college graduates are ready for the workplace. Who am I to disagree with their research; after earning a Bachelor and two Masters Degrees, I wasn't ready… I have addressed well over 1,000 students. Many of them are following the same advice I listened to at their age, "*Go to class, work hard and get a good education, then once you graduate, you will get a good job.*" I can say without reservations, *"these students are no more prepared to enter the work force than I was 30 years earlier."*

Many employers feel most young workers are ill-prepared for the workplace. They say far too many new employees have problems following instructions, lack a positive attitude, communicate poorly and frequently come to work late.

This is why I wrote this book; to teach people how to avoid making the mistakes I made early in my career. My research was conducted over a period of twenty five years and includes observations of, and interactions with executives in all phases of business. This book is designed to be a guide for anyone looking to successfully navigate corporate culture.

Learn to avoid orientation errors, workplace miss-steps, boardroom blunders and career altering landmines. There's an old saying, *"A smart man learns from his mistakes, but a wise man learns from someone else's mistakes... and a fool never learns!"* For the record, I've made more than my share of mistakes, so… **Read this book and become wise.**

ARE YOU SOFT?

SOFT SKILLS ARE THE HARD SKILLS OF THE 21ST CENTURY WORKFORCE AND MILLIONS OF YOUNG PEOPLE LACK WHAT IT TAKES TO PARTICIPATE!

Schools, communities and corporations can no longer afford to focus on academic outcomes alone. Soft skills are essential to personal career success and to the success of corporate America. Our young people will soon be part of the global economy and therefore the global workforce. If they are unable to compete in this economy it will have menacing repercussions for America's economic leadership and prosperity. Technical skills are no longer enough, you need to successfully communicate in order to build relationships and collaborations in today's workforce. Unfortunately, these skills are often undervalued by employers who expect people to already know how to perform on the job.

Some enlightened employers look to the future with anxiety as they realize the need to make significant financial investments in remedial training for those who enter the workforce without the skills their company will need.

Don't take my word for it; listen to the experts. You will be surprised at how few of America's youth are equipped with the "soft" skills necessary to effectively compete. The research is immense and conclusive…

According to **Are They Ready to Work;** a report commissioned by the business sector, three-quarters of employers say incoming high school graduates are deficient in "applied skills." These deficits are apparent across all lines of race and ethnicity, education levels and family income. Almost all young Americans today are at risk of entering the workforce without enough of the skills that make for success.

Additionally, 40% of employers said the high school graduates they hire lack enough of the "soft" skills they need for entry-level jobs.

The **America's Promise Alliance's** Every Child, Every Promise report, states, that growing attention to test scores and graduation rates, leads policymakers and practitioners to overlook other, equally significant ways in which we are short-changing young people.

Specifically, a large percentage of the children and youth who will enter the work force over the next two decades are lacking enough of the "soft" or applied skills — such as teamwork, decision-making, and communication — that will help them become effective employees and managers.

According to **Economist and Nobel laureate Dr. James Heckman**, soft skills are just as essential to a young person's success as the more frequently cited academic indicators. They are essential prerequisites for high school graduates to enter the workforce successfully.

Psychologist and author Daniel Goleman, brings together years of research to show that soft skills matter twice as much as technical skills in job success. His data from more than 500 organizations is the foundation of the best-selling book, Emotional Intelligence. He proves factors such as integrity, self-awareness; self-confidence, self-control, and commitment create more successful employees and more successful companies.

An **American Express** study found over 60 percent of their managers agreed soft skills were the most important traits considered when evaluating an employee's performance.

A **Seattle Jobs Initiative** survey found:

- Soft skills are the most important attribute – and the most difficult to find – among entry-level job applications.
- 75% of employers said soft skills were as important as – or more important than – technical skills in securing entry level employment.
- 67% of area employers believe that the educational system has an important role in the development of soft skills.

- The top response from employers regarding who is responsible for soft skills development was "employees themselves."

The majority of employers feel the responsibility of gaining these skills is the employees. I don't know about you, but when I was in college there wasn't an option to take a "soft skills" course during registration.

The **Gallup Poll/Phi Delta Kappa annual survey** on Americans' attitudes toward public education found, Most Americans believe schools should teach "soft skills."

- 80% of adults "strongly agree" that K-12 schools should teach critical thinking to students.
- 78% of Americans "strongly agree" that schools should teach students communication skills.

Americans' believe students should be better equipped to analyze information, communicate effectively and to collaborate with diverse people in a global work environment to solve complex problems.

A **Wall Street Journal/Harris Interactive poll** found that employers are seeking managers with 'soft' skills and believe MBA programs should devote even more attention to them. In fact, prestigious business schools, such as Yale, MIT, Vanderbilt and Carnegie Mellon are following suit.

If you didn't attend a prestigious business school, this book is for you! I learned the 'Soft Skills' from the University of Life and experience has often been cited as the best teacher. One of my students forwarded the following comparison of the value of 'Soft Skills'.

"To secure and maintain a job you naturally need a range of technical skills. Dentists need to know how to fill cavities. Secretaries need to type 100+ words per minute. Accountants need to be certified.

Beyond the technical skills, which dentist do you go to? The one who is pleasant and takes time to answer your questions; or the one who treats you like a number in a long line of numbered mouths? Which secretary do you retain when times are lean? The one whose attitude is positive and upbeat, and who is always willing to help; or the one who is inflexible and has a hard time admitting mistakes?

Likewise, think about accountants. The one who has a great work ethic and encourages his colleagues is the one who will, most likely, excel in his position and organization. In these situations, and all the others like them, it's the soft skills that matter."

Technical skills will get you in the door, but once you're in the room, it's your people skills that will open the doors that follow. Your communication skills, attitude and work ethic are crucial for career success.

Step 1:
P.I.E. Theory…

IF YOU'RE NOT AT THE TABLE, YOU'RE ON THE MENU!

Most new entrants into the workplace desire to move up-the-ladder as fast as they possibly can. This common objective to *'get–to-the-top'* often serves as the spawning ground for unhealthy competition. Far too many believe the only way to stand out is to pull others down. Regrettably, for many employers, rivalries create unpleasant work environments, weak teams, and lower levels of productivity. All of these factors contribute to high employee turnover rates.

The PIE Theory is a proven method that ensures you are in the right lane in the *'race-to-the-top'*. You won't have to step over anybody to get ahead so you can be the unifying force within your office. I learned this philosophy from a senior executive at the bank one evening shortly after the brown suit debacle.

One day Phil, a senior officer at the bank, asked if I could meet with him after work. Of course I said yes, when someone on his level asks to meet, you don't refuse. But to be honest, I was annoyed because I had plans, his meeting would make me late for 'happy hour.' I thought, *"Why couldn't we meet during the day??? This was my time; I was off the clock!"*

Everyone else was headed out of the building and I was headed up the elevator to Phil's office. As soon as I stepped in the room he started the meeting. The first thing he did was compliment my suit. *"Paul, that's a nice looking suit you're wearing. You look real professional."* The suit was new, in fact, it was the first time I had worn it. I was flattered by his commendation and thought, *"Oh yeah, I'm projecting power and leadership!"*

Truthfully, the outfit I was wearing, the jacket, shirt, tie and handkerchief was an exact replica of the combination I saw the bank president wear during an executive coffee with the trainees. I liked the way his red tie contrasted with his crisp white shirt. It was framed by a navy blue suit with a white handkerchief in the coat pocket. His look was the embodiment of power.

That was the first time I met him and he left an indelible impression on me. He looked in charge and personified leadership. It has been said that imitation is the sincerest form of flattery; well… he did such a great job coordinating his outfit that I copied it.

Phil changed the conversation and started talking about a company event held a week earlier. He shared a few personal stories then asked if I had a good time. The truth; I didn't go; I went to the movies that evening. I thought about saying, *YES; "There were over 500 people at that event, he wouldn't know if I wasn't there*???"

But honesty has always been my policy, so I told him the truth; I didn't attend.

He walked over to the white board drew a large circle and asked, *"Have you ever heard of the PIE Theory?* I responded, *"NO!"* He continued, *"It's a concept for advancement, a philosophy I live by. I've used it for over thirty years and I credit a large portion of my success to its principles."* He then began to teach, *"The 'P' stands for Productivity. The 'I' stands for Image and the 'E' stands for Exposure. These are three essential elements for climbing the corporate ladder.*"

He continued, *"What percentage of a person's success would you credit to their productivity?* I answered, "*at least 85%! You have to be able to do your job well."* He took his marker and drew a pie slice that composed 85% of the circle and then placed a 'P' in the center. He asked, *"How much would you credit to their Image;"* and I told him 10%. He marked out 10% of the circle, placed an 'I' in the center and then put an 'E' in the middle of the 5% remainder.

He said, *"Most people are like you, they think doing a great job is all it takes to make it to the top of their profession. I understand the rationale; you work hard, outperform your peers and you will receive the benefits of your labor. It makes sense; unfortunately that is not how it works in the real world.*

When a company hires you, they assume you have the talent and capacity to perform the requirements of the job. You will be trained and after training you will be expected to complete assignments. Performance is an expectation; it's the quid-pro-quo for hiring you! Productivity is only 40% of the equation."

Image is 30% because it is extremely important to know the culture of your organization. Every team has a uniform. Look at sports teams; it doesn't matter if its college or professional they wear the same uniform. Look at policemen, firemen or any branch of the military, every team has a uniform that reflects the culture of that organization. In banking, our culture is conservative. We want people to trust us with their life savings; it is important to convey stability and competency to build trust. The preferred colors in our industry are navy blue and grey. I can tell by the suit you are wearing that you understand the dress code.

Exposure is the other 30% of the equation. It is extremely important to have the look that represents the culture of your team, but it is equally important for that Image to be seen! Having the perfect image and keeping it hidden in your office will not advance your cause. <u>People hire and promote those</u>

that they know, trust and like. It is impossible for people to get to know you if you keep your nose on the grindstone and never meet the other members of your team. Coffee breaks, luncheons, after work cocktails and weekend get-togethers are settings in which people are informally selected for advancement." He then said, *"Paul, your absence was noted last week."*

He taught me a very important lesson. Phil invited me to his office to let me know missing company functions was not increasing my chances of moving up the corporate ladder.

After making his point, he asked what my plans were for the evening. I told him about happy hour and he asked if I would join him for a cocktail before I left. I really wanted to meet my friends, but when someone on his level invites you for a cocktail... I accepted his invitation and we headed to the Press Club.

The Press Club was a private Club on the top floor of the building. Membership was one of the perks at the bank. Every officer was granted a Press Club membership. This was my first time in the club and the first thing I noticed was the large number of patrons who were bank executives. Apparently the Press Club was a popular spot for bank leadership after work. A couple of my classmates from the trainee program were there also! They never mentioned the Press Club during any of our team building sessions.

Phil was one of the highest ranking officials in the bank, so eventually everyone made their way over to our table, even the trainees. Phil introduced me to each person who approached and many of them were interested in conversing with me; no doubt they wondered what my connection was to Phil.

Phil was showing me how the P.I.E. Theory worked in real time. A few more compliments on my suit affirmed I was portraying the proper corporate image. Phil knew the image was right and he invited me to the Press Club to get the right exposure. Even though I wasn't a member of the Press Club, the reception I received made me feel like one...

That one event turned out to be the combination that unlocked the door of access. From that day forward, those executives began to speak to me and treat me with familiarity. I received lunch invitations and was invited back to the Club. The P.I.E. Theory worked! I saw with my own eyes that exposing the correct image can create a competitive advantage. People sized me up based on how I looked and carried myself; my appearance enabled me to gain access into management circles.

I began to build relationships with executives throughout the bank. I systematically met with every executive Phil introduced. It's a smart move to build relationships with the people who are on top of their game in your organization. I invited them to coffee, lunch or cocktails. It was to my advantage to build an expansive network throughout the bank. At the end of each meeting I asked who they thought I should be meeting with and then I would schedule meetings with them.

A couple of months later I followed up with Phil to share with him how well the P.I.E. Theory was working. I was astute enough to wear another dark blue suit. Phil was captivated with my approach to developing relationships within the bank. In fact, he was so impressed that he granted me full access to his Press Club membership!

Only bank officers were awarded memberships. I now had a convenient location for lunch, dinner and after work cocktails, on Phil's tab… Within a 20 minute meeting, my quality of life elevated! Because of the P.I.E. Theory I officially moved up a rung on the proverbial ladder of success.

One afternoon I invited my entire trainee class to lunch. Yes, those same people who went to lunch without me on the first day. The total price of the meal was about $119 dollars; the look on their faces when I signed the tab, PRICELESS...

Step 2:
The Executive Handshake

When Phil entered a room, he owned it. He walked through the door and took the initiative to greet everyone; even those he didn't know. It seemed like he was on a mission to personally interact with as many people as possible. Phil led with authority and confidence, the Executive Handshake was the weapon he used to own the moment.

I knew the handshake was an important introductory tool used to seal deals and contracts, but Phil appeared to gain more from the exchange. He seemed to transfer positive energy to people; they were energized after shaking his hand.

When I asked Phil about his entrance and penchant for flesh pressing, he explained *"Judgments are made about people based on how they shake hands. Your character and trustworthiness are assessed based on that brief moment of touch. Many offers have been withheld, promotions have been denied, and opportunities have been missed simply because someone didn't shake hands properly. When you shake hands you're saying more than "hello," you're saying "this is who I am."*

The first impression begins with a handshake and it sets the tone for the rest of the meeting. People with firm handshakes are generally more extroverted than those with limp handshakes. Firm hand shakers are considered more hirable by interviewers and people with 'wimpy' shakes are judged to be more timid and less impressive.

Watching Phil I began to realize the power in his handshake; something so simple placed him in a position of authority. I had never looked at the handshake as a tool for success, so I began to study him to learn how to use the handshake to advance my career. I realized properly administering this handshake could be beneficial to my upward mobility.

I coined his handshake the Executive Handshake because it was the same handshake I encountered every time I had an interaction with an executive. It was unlike the handshake I used with my college friends and it was quite different from the creative handshakes we made when I was a kid. I labeled the essential elements of the Executive Handshake and have been teaching them to students from elementary school to college for decades. The following Six Steps make the Executive Handshake:

1. Good Posture
2. Eye Contact
3. Shoot from the Hip
4. Go to the Thumb Pocket

5. Give a Firm Squeeze
6. Lean forward

President John F. Kennedy commissioned a study to determine the most effective handshake. According to an article in the DAILY MIND, “Kennedy knew he would be shaking hands with the world’s most powerful men and women and as such he wanted to get it right.

John F. Kennedy was in power during a time of worldwide nuclear uncertainty and he understood the importance of a handshake. A weak handshake with a Cuban or Soviet dignitary could create great problems for the United States. A strong handshake, on the other hand, could convey confidence, stability and trustworthiness and open up new dialogues and friendships between leaders that have long been opponents.

If you are a business person your handshake can be the maker or breaker of a big contract or deal. If you are a doctor or health care provider your handshake can fill a patient with confidence and trust. It is extremely important for all people, regardless of your race or way of life, to learn how to shake hands with meaning.

JFK’s study found that the most effective handshake was the “double handshake” where the left hand is placed under the right hand to “cup” the clasped hands. Positioning the left hand in this way adds an extra dimension of enthusiasm to the shake and conveys a great sense of friendship and trust in the other person.

However, the actual shaking of the hands is only a small part of the business of shaking hands. Here are a few tips on how you can make the perfect handshake:

1. Look the person in the eyes

There is a substantial amount of research showing that good eye contact increases feelings of trust. Looking the person in the eyes shows that you are engaging them. It shows that you are interested in this meeting and you are glad to see them. Making eye contact as you approach lets the person know you want to interact.

The position of your eyes is almost as important as the hands themselves. Many leading business people say your eyes convey the most about you during that initial point of contact. If you look down toward the ground you are telling the person that you are shy, nervous and possibly untrustworthy. Avoiding eye contact is behavior typically seen in someone who has done something wrong and feels ashamed or guilty.

Men need to extend the eye contact for at least three seconds without blinking or looking away as they shake hands. Women need to be careful of holding eye contact for more than three to five seconds at a time with men they have not met because men may perceive extended eye contact as a sexual advance.

2. Use a firm grip

Another key element of a good handshake is a firm grip; academic research shows a firm handshake indicates confidence, strength and vigor. It shows you are open to involvement and you are committed to being there. The pressure should be equal or slightly more than the pressure you are given. Never squeeze the other's hand to see who can hold the hardest or longest. The rule is to match the pressure or add no more than two degrees of force.

People may perceive a soft grip to mean you are weak of character or not really interested in meeting them.

3. Don't be too hasty

A handshake should be inviting but not rushed. When you rush a handshake you inevitably get caught in that embarrassingly halfhearted position where neither person is really gripping properly. When you go in for a handshake offer your hand with your fingers straight and your thumb high and make sure you do not grip until the person's thumb is firmly locked next to yours.

You should also not be too hasty in letting go. "*If you can't even shake my hand how can we develop a trusting relationship?*" Make sure you hold on long enough to show the person that you are excited to meet them.

4. Don't shake too much

One of the worst handshakes you can get is the one where the person shakes your arm like they are trying to tear it off. It is fine to do two or three small shakes but that is enough. Too much shaking can convey over-excitement and in some cases it gives the impression that you are desperate.

5. Make correct use of the left hand

JFK thought the best place for the left hand was cupped under the shaking hands. However, this might not always be appropriate. The JFK cupped left hand is really quite an intimate grip. It's something you would do to someone you really admire or an old business friend that you haven't seen in years. JFK correctly used it on foreign leaders, party donors, etc.

But sometimes the "correct" use of the left hand is not to use it at all. You will find yourself in certain situations where it might not be appropriate to do anything other than give a quick shake with your right hand. Make sure you use your own intelligence to determine the best use of the left hand. One place where the JFK shake is really very good is when you have just reached an agreement or a deal with a person and you want to express your happiness."

Once I discovered President Kennedy put this much thought into the handshake, I looked for more research to validate the positive power of the handshake. I was amazed when I discovered there was scientific data to support the Executive Handshake I created almost 30 years ago!

According to Body Language Expert Patti Wood, *"Few things create such an effective first impression as an easily given, gracious handshake. But unless your father took you aside and gave you tips as a teenager, most likely no one told you the ideal way to shake hands."* Based on her research, here is the best way to execute the **'perfect handshake'** by American standards.

- Rise, if seated. This rule used to apply to men only; now women should rise as well. If you remain seated when someone is introduced to you, the communication of personal indifference is unmistakable, not to mention offensive. The only approved exception to rising to shake hands is if you are eating. If that is the case, you can wait to shake hands until after you are done.

- Walk up to the person with confidence. Keep your head level and your hands at your side. Be sure to keep your hands out of your pockets. Research indicates that we don't trust people with hands in their pockets. Make sure your right hand is free to shake hands. Always shift any purses, briefcases, papers, beverages or cell phones to your left hand before you begin the greeting.

- Face the person heart-to-heart. When you stand at an angle and don't face the person squarely, you are sending the symbolic message that you are not being straight and open. You may look as if you need to protect yourself, you do not like the other person, or you feel the need to reduce the intimacy or the duration of the interaction.

- If you have a problem with clammy hands, don't forget to wipe them on your handkerchief or tissue before you shake hands. And at social functions, carry any iced drinks in your left hand, so your right hand will not be cold and damp when a handshake is called for.

- Reach out your right hand and arm across your body to your right. The forcefulness and confidence of the move lets the other person know you not only want to shake hands, you look forward to it.

- Make sure the arm goes fully outward as an arm held closely to the body indicates timidity and lack of confidence.

- Make sure your hand is straight up with the thumb on top. The thumb on top is symbolic; it indicates you want equality in your interaction. No one person will dominate. You will respect the other person and expect him or her to respect you.

- Stretch out and open your hand between the thumb and the first finger so that you slide your hand easily into the web of the other person's hand. Make sure the rest of your fingers are together with your palm flat rather than cupped so your palm can touch their palm...

- Make palm-to-palm contact. Open palms symbolically show a desire to be open and honest in your interactions; not giving a person contact with your palm in a handshake is read subliminally as a lack of openness and honesty. It's why we hate a wimpy or limp handshake. It makes the other person nervous and he or she may wonder what you are hiding.

- The most important thing to remember when shaking someone's hand is their name. ALWAYS call them by their name and never use lazy substitutes like "man" or "dude". People love to hear their own name. When you shake a person's hand and greet them by their name you are effectively saying "you are important enough to me that I bothered to remember your name".

When you use your speech in conjunction with the handshake you are interacting with the person physically, verbally and emotionally. A triple header handshake like this leaves an impression.

Remind people of your name straight away as you shake their hand. It is important to realize that other people want to remember your name just as much as you want to remember theirs – nobody likes forgetting a name. If you have met a person before try to give them a little reminder as you shake their hand. You could say something like, *"Paul Bryant, Great to see you again John."* This will help to put them at ease and hopefully make the meeting a little more streamlined.

Why do we shake hands?

Handshakes started with the Roman arm clasp. One man would reach out his right hand, his weapon hand, and clasp just below the elbow of the man he was greeting. With this greeting neither person could wield a weapon easily. Medieval knights created the shaking part of the handshake because they knew that other knights hid daggers up in their sleeves and that the shaking would dislodge any hidden weapons. So basically handshakes are weapons checks: *"Are you packing any weapons? Let me check. Nope. Okay, let's talk."*

The blades of jealousy envy and deceit can be as damaging to your career as a dagger to the back of a medieval knight. When navigating the workplace you need as many allies as possible. The Executive handshake is the fastest, most effective way to establish relationships. Increase your chances of making friends and influencing people. The Executive Handshake is a valuable arrow you must have in your corporate quiver.

The handshake is extremely important to our society. Peace treaties have been promised over a handshake. Wars have been ended by a handshake. Great business deals have begun because of a good handshake. Make sure you follow the tips above whenever you shake someone's hand. A good handshake is a first impression that will last a long time in person's mind.

Step 3:
SPAM

DO NOT DELETE!

Phil was like a politician on the campaign trail, he charmed every person he met. It didn't matter if it was an executive or a janitor; he had an optimistic encouraging word for everyone.

I decided to emulate Phil's Human Relations Skills. I copied the President's wardrobe and it worked; I used the P.I.E. Theory and it worked, I figured the third time would be a charm. I made a habit of presenting the most positive personality possible. My goal was to uplift everyone I encountered. I took the initiative to say something inspiring to everyone; my goal was to leave people feeling better than they did before we met. I gave a generous portion of S.P.A.M. to everybody!

I know SPAM carries a negative meaning. You stop opening email from people who send SPAM. You defriend Spammers! However the SPAM I'm referring to is different; it is difficult to refuse. If you give someone a generous dose of my SPAM I guarantee they won't defriend you.

The SPAM I'm talking about stands for:

Smile **P**ositive **A**ttitude and **M**anners

SMILE - I began to greet everyone with a warm and friendly smile. A smile is the key that fits the lock to everyone's heart. It's the universal welcome; it makes people feel comfortable. I found that when I smiled, people usually smiled back. And people look better when they smile; it's like they say, *"If you look good, you feel good."* So smiling at people not only lifted their spirits, it raised my spirits as well.

Mother Teresa said, "Peace begins with a smile. So let us always meet each other with smile, for the smile is the beginning of love. We shall never know all the good that a simple smile can do."

A considerable amount of research has been conducted on the positive attributes of the smile. From the Huffington Post and the Psychological Association of Research to the Harvard Business Review, all speak of the positive aspects of smiling. The following summaries list some of their findings:

"Smiling stimulates our brain's reward mechanisms in a way that even chocolate, a well-regarded pleasure-inducer, cannot match. Smiling seems to give us the same happiness that exercising induces in terms of how our brain responds. In short: our brain feels good and tells us to smile; we smile and tell our brain it feels good and so forth."

Your brain keeps track of your smiles, kind of like a smile scorecard. It knows how often you've smiled and which overall emotional state you are in therefore. Smiling reduces stress that your body and mind feel, almost similar to getting good sleep. Smiling helps to generate more positive emotions within you, that's why we often feel happier around children – they smile more.

Smiling decreases the stress-induced hormones that negatively affect your physical and mental health. According to many experts, smiling is not only an outward manifestation of happy feelings; it may actually cause happy feelings. According to this hypothesis, the facial changes involved in smiling have direct effects on certain brain activities associated with happiness. In a yearbook study, researchers tracked the lives of women who had the best smiles in their yearbook photos. They discovered women who smiled the most lived happier lives, had happier marriages and had fewer setbacks.

POSITIVE ATTITUDE – An equal amount of study has been conducted on the attributes of an optimistic temperament. Studies show positive attitudes pay dividends in health, life expectancy, career success and higher scores on achievement tests. The Journal of Personality and Social Psychology reported that optimists handle stress better than pessimists. "*Optimists respond to disappointments like being turned down for a job by formulating a plan of action and asking other people for help and advice; pessimists more often react to such difficulties by trying to forget the whole thing or assuming there is nothing they can do to change things.*"

Another study found optimistic salesmen sold 37 percent more insurance in their first two years; and pessimists were twice as likely to quit in their first year.

I made a habit of offering sincere appreciation and encouragement to my co-workers. I became a desired team member because I always bought sunshine into the room. People looked forward to my presence and when I spoke they listened.

It's been said that 'opposites attract;' I disagree; especially when it comes to success and achievement. Winners surround themselves with winners and successful people like to be around other successful people. The law of attraction says whatever you send out into the universe, the universe will send back to you. If you want positive uplifting relationships, you must present yourself as a positive uplifting person.

The Press Club experience revealed to me how the workplace will pay dividends to those able to attract successful people. I know the reception I received from those executives was because they met me through Phil. If you are looking to progress within your company you should learn this lesson immediately. *"Who you hang around says who you are..."*

MANNERS – I grew up in the *"Please and Thank you"* generation. My parents made certain we were respectful and used good manners. *"Yes Ma'am, No Sir"* were commonly used when addressing elders. I remember the look on my mother's face when someone told her, *"Your children are so well behaved."* She was humbled by the compliment and would later tell us how proud she was. Now that I'm a parent, I understand her feelings. Not only were those kudos recognition of her children, they were a also a reflection of her parenting. I can't think of any parent who does not like to hear positive comments about their children?

Employers, Managers, Bosses and Co-Workers are no different! They like being around decent, respectful people; we feel good when pleasant things are said about the people close to us. How many times has someone accomplished something great and you've heard someone say, *"I know her, or I work with him, or they live in my neighborhood."*

Good manners, is a method to show respect and consideration for others. Exceptional manners will help you build relationships with everyone you encounter. The internet is full of tips on how to use good manners. The following are several my students sent to me worth sharing:

1. Practice courtesy. Say *"please"* and *"thank you,"* when you need to, even to the person behind the counter at McDonald's. People notice when you're courteous and respectful toward them. Additionally, say "excuse me" whenever you accidentally bump into someone, or if you need to leave a social setting temporarily.

2. Hold open doors for other people. If someone will be entering the door shortly after you, pause a second and hold it open. Say *"After you, sir/ma'am,"* if the person is a stranger; if not, use his or her name in place of sir or ma'am. If you're unsure about whether or not the other person would appreciate having the door held open, ask politely. Say, *"May I get the door for you?"* This gives the other person an opportunity to accept or decline. And ladies, you don't have to be a guy to hold a door open.

3. Speak politely. Keep the volume of your voice as low as possible while still allowing people to hear you, and don't use slang or filler words (such as "like," "uh," "so..." and so on).

- Don't discuss rude topics, such as bodily functions, gossip, dirty jokes, or swear words.

- Don't interrupt or override another person when he or she is speaking. Practice being a good listener, and talk when it's your turn.

4. Give up your seat on public transportation. If you're on a crowded train or bus and you notice someone struggling to stand up (such as an elderly person, a pregnant woman, or someone with a lot of parcels), offer your seat. Saying something like, *"Sir, I'd be delighted if you'd accept my seat"* can make the situation less awkward for the other person. If he or she declines, be gracious; say, "*Please feel welcome to let me know if you change your mind."*

5. Congratulate people. Offer your congratulations to someone who's just made a big accomplishment (such as graduating or being promoted), has added to his or her family (such as getting married or having a child), or has otherwise done something worthy of praise.

- Be a good sport. Congratulate anyone who beats you in a race, sporting event, election or other competition.

6. Be a courteous driver. Driving with good manners might seem outdated, but it's actually a matter of safety. Try to follow these tips:

- If you come to a four-way stop that another driver doesn't seem to know how to manage, just motion him or her to go ahead of you.

- Yield to pedestrians, and try to give cyclists plenty of room. Remember, your two-ton vehicle is a lot more dangerous to them than they are to you, so it's your responsibility to try to make sure everyone is safe.
- Don't tailgate people or refuse to let them into your lane.
- Use your turn signals even if you don't think anyone is around - you never know if there's a pedestrian or cyclist you just can't see.

7. Know how to greet people. Whether you're in an informal or formal situation, acknowledging the presence of another person is a fundamental point of having good manners. (Failing to do so can be seen as an insult in most settings.) Here's what to do:

- If you're greeting someone you know as a family member or close friend, an informal greeting is enough. It can be as simple as *"Hey, how's it going?"*
- If you're greeting someone who's an elder, business associate, church leader, or other formal acquaintance, stick to a formal greeting unless you're instructed to do otherwise. Greet the other person using his or her title (such as *"Mrs. Jones" or "Pastor Smith"*), or use *"sir"* or *"ma'am."* Avoid slang such as *"hey"* or *"hi,"* and try to speak in full sentences. Something like, *"Hello, Mrs. Jones. How are you today?"* could be appropriate.

- Make necessary greeting gestures. For informal greetings, how you physically interact with that person is your choice - you could do nothing at all, or offer a hug, handshake, or other greeting based on your relationship with that person. For formal greetings, it's appropriate to offer a handshake. If the person you're greeting formally goes in for a hug accept it graciously

8. Manage introductions with grace. If you're with two people who don't know each other, but you know both of them, it's your responsibility to make the introduction. Follow these steps:

The person who is of higher social rank should have the second person introduced to him or her. That is, the person of lower rank is the one who should be presented to the person of higher rank. (For example, "Mrs. Jones, I'd like to introduce you to my good friend, Jessica Smith." Jessica is the person of lower rank in this introduction.) This is relatively easy in some situations, but here are some guidelines for when it's less clear-cut: younger people should be presented to elders, men should be presented to women, and laypeople should be presented to clergy, public servants, and members of the military to people of higher rank.

Start out an introduction by naming the person of higher rank, then say *"I'd like to introduce you to..." or "this is..."*, and name the person of lower rank.

After the two people have greeted each other, offer some information about each person. For instance, you might say, "I've known Jessica since grade school" or "Mrs. Jones is my mother's dear friend." Whatever you say should be able to start or sustain a short conversation; which you're responsible for carrying.

When you're being introduced to someone, look that person in the eyes and remember their name. After the introduction, greet the other person and say something like *"It's a pleasure to meet you,"* and offer a handshake.

9. Write thank-you notes. Whenever anyone gives you a gift or does something particularly nice for you, send them a thank-you note within a few days. Note how thankful you are for the specific gift or action, and how delighted you are to have the other person's friendship.

- Note that a thank-you email can be appropriate in certain situations, such as the workplace or for someone who lives so far away that an email is much more expedient.

Dining Manners

1. Don't chew with your mouth open. It's an obvious rule, but one that's easy to forget when you're enjoying a delicious meal.

2. Say *"excuse me"* whenever you need to leave the table.

3. Ask for someone to pass you a dish or a seasoning. Never reach across a dish or someone else's plate to reach something; instead, politely ask the person sitting next to you to *"please pass the sauce."*

4. Don't put your elbows on the table when you're eating. If the meal has yet to begin or is over, however, putting your elbows on the table is acceptable.

5. How you hold your utensils probably depends on where you come from. Both are perfectly appropriate. In general, there are two styles:

    a. American style: If you're cutting food, you'll transfer the fork to your non-dominant hand and put the knife in your dominant hand. After the food is cut, you'll lay down the blade of the knife on the edge of the plate, and switch the fork back to your dominant hand to move the food to your mouth.

    b. Continental style: The fork remains in the left hand, while you use the right hand to hold the knife and cut your food. Once you're done cutting, you might lay the blade of the knife on the edge of the plate, or just keep the knife in your hand.

6. How you put your utensils on your plate communicates to the service staff whether you're finished eating or you still plan to continue. For the purpose of these instructions, imagine the dinner plate like it's the face of a clock.

    a. If you're finished eating, lay your fork and knife side-by side so that the prongs and blade are slightly above the center of the plate, and so that the handles are pointing between 3 and 4 o'clock.

    b. If you plan to continue eating, lay down your fork and knife so that the prongs and blade are near the center, with the handle of one utensil pointing at 8 o'clock and the handle of the other pointing at 4 o'clock.

7. One of the most intimidating parts about dining can be, not knowing which utensils or plates to use. Here's a quick primer:

    If you forget the particulars, remember: "work from the outside in." This basically means that if there are utensils on both the right and left sides of the plate, you'll start with what's furthest right and furthest left, and gradually work closer to the plate.

If all else fails, just watch what everyone else is doing.

The Place Setting

You should have a dinner plate in the center. Immediately to the left of the plate will be two forks -- the one closest to the plate is the "dinner fork," to be used for the main course; the one furthest from the plate is meant for a salad or appetizer.

A dinner knife will be directly to the right of the plate, with the blade facing toward it; next to that will be two spoons. The soup spoon is furthest to the right; the dessert spoon (or teaspoon) is between the soup spoon and the knife.

Your glass should be positioned directly above the dinner knife. Subsequent glasses should be placed to the right according to type in a formal place setting. The one directly above your dinner knife is your water glass; to the right of that is a wine glass, and then a sherry glass to the far right.

You might have a small salad plate to the left of the forks.

You might have a small bread plate to the upper-left of the dinner plate, with a small butter knife. Use the butter knife to take a pat of butter and put it on your plate; then use the knife to spread "your" butter onto the bread.

A dessert spoon or fork might be placed horizontally above the dinner plate. A coffee cup and saucer should be placed just above and to the right of the knife and spoons.

Phone Etiquette

1. Only use your cell phone in appropriate settings. For instance, it's impolite to use it in the bathroom, in the middle of a meeting, when a service person is helping you, in church, or (sometimes) on public transportation. If you feel awkward using it or people are giving you dirty looks, you should probably put it away. When talking on the phone in a public space, keep in mind that everything you say is no longer just your news. Keep your voice at an "indoor" level. Generally, people with good manners don't talk about embarrassing private issues in public.

2. When on the phone, don't talk with others in the room. Nothings worse than having a phone conversation with someone who chats, perhaps not listening to what you're saying, and you can't tell if they are speaking to you or others. If someone tries to talk to you, simply point to your phone and they will get the message.

3. Avoid using the computer while on the phone unless it's part of customer services. It is extremely rude and unpleasant when someone makes you listen to a clacking keyboard.

4. When with others in a social setting, try to refrain from using your cell phone. It implies you'd rather be somewhere else, with someone else, and that who you are with is less important.

5. Avoid calling people during meals, work, and school unless in an emergency. People don't expect you to drop in and visit at these times, unless it is arranged, so don't drop in via your telephone. This includes texting also.

6. Ensure the number you have is correct. If you do disturb someone and it's the wrong number then 'please' have the decency to say, *"I'm so sorry! I have the wrong number!"* DO NOT just hang up. That

individual may be ill, in a wheelchair, or elderly, etc., so you should show respect and apologize for their inconvenience. Likewise, if a person with a wrong number phoned you, politely point out that they have called the wrong number.

7. Check your voice! It carries much more than just a tone, and reflects your character and personality even on the phone! Remember: your listener cannot see you, so your phone-voice becomes your facial expressions, gestures, personality, and character. Always check your voice when speaking; speak in a pleasant tone and very clearly. Smile through your voice! What they hear will make a positive or negative impression.

8. Practice basic conversational courtesy. When someone answers the phone don't be harsh and abrupt by telling them what you want first. It gives the wrong impression before you start! And don't say, *"Who is this?"* You phoned them, so introduce yourself and state who you are and what you want – politely!

9. Give people a chance to answer their phone! They could be outside in their garden, knitting, baking, washing the car, or at another end of the house. Don't just ring three times and hang up! It's annoying

when you stopped doing something and just as the phone gets to your ear the caller hangs up!

10. Don't spend hours chatting to someone. Don't waste people's time or disturb the household! It's one of the biggest turn-off's to having a friendly chat! They will not want to talk to you again.

11. Know how to answer the phone. Just be pleasant and polite and say, *"Hello."* Avoid saying, *"Good afternoon, Bryant residence"* or *"Paul Bryant speaking."*

12. If the call is for someone else, say something such as; *"One moment please, I'll go and get them for you."* Put the receiver down gently. If who they want to speak to is unavailable, say, *"I'm sorry, Robin isn't available right now. May I take a message for her and ask her to phone you as soon as she can?"*

13. Put someone on hold politely. If you must carry on two conversations at once you should always excuse yourself from one and resume it later. Say, *"I'm sorry, can you hold on a minute; my boss is telling me something,"* and wait for the person's answer. If the personal conversation will last more than a minute, it would be better to ask, *"Can I call you back? The President*

needs to talk to me and it may take a few minutes."

If you need a restroom break, say something to get off the phone, without sharing too much information. All you need to say is *"Can you hold on for a few minutes? I will be right back."*

There is also a right and wrong way for using technology at work. Don't use your company computer for personal use, or text during meetings. The Computer Ethics Institute developed the Ten Commandments of Computer Ethics to address the gray area between the ethical and unethical use of computer technology. These will help you determine what is acceptable.

1. Thou shalt not use a computer to harm other people.

2. Thou shalt not interfere with other people's computer work.

3. Thou shalt not snoop around in other people's files.

4. Thou shalt not use a computer to steal.

5. Thou shalt not use a computer to bear false witness.

6. Thou shalt not use or copy software for which you have not paid.

7. Thou shalt not use other people's computer resources without authorization.

8. Thou shalt not appropriate other people's intellectual output.

9. Thou shalt think about the social consequences of the program you write.

10. Thou shalt use a computer in ways that show consideration and respect.

Step 4:
(B.R.E.)

BOARD ROOM ETIQUETTE

The Management Trainee position was a coveted job within the bank. We were able to develop relationships with the leadership in every area of the organization. The program lasted 18 months and provided participants with a total immersion into the world of banking. We spent 45 days in each division gaining an overall understanding of every position. We received high exposure to senior level management.

Our mission was to look as impressive as possible in every division. We were rated by each division manager and were positioning ourselves for job offers after graduation. In essence, we had a 45 day interview with the leadership in every department.

We had full access to ALL meetings and conferences. At times this was very exciting; how many people have the opportunity to sit in loan committee meetings to see first-hand what it takes to get million dollar deals approved. But at other times those meetings were long and boring; there is nothing more tedious than a 90 minute meeting on compliance.

The last thing any trainee wanted to do was to fall asleep during a meeting. According to trainee folklore, one trainee fell asleep during a meeting. When that meeting ended, everyone left him in the conference room sleeping. He was awakened 20 minutes later by the people with the next reservation for the room; one of them happened to be the President of the bank. I can only imagine his humiliation; waking up to find the president of the bank looking him in the face.

His story traveled through the grape vine and followed him as he moved throughout the bank. When he graduated from the program he didn't receive a management job offer. The race-to-the-top for his executive career stalled before it had a chance to get started. His only job offer was for a drive through teller position in a remote branch of the bank.

This story was told to incentivize trainees to stay alert during meetings. It was definitely a motivator; however, I still found it difficult to stay focused during meetings that lasted over and hour. We only attend meetings in an observatory capacity and weren't expected to contribute. So it often amounted to nothing more than sitting in a room and looking interested while people discussed issues we knew little about.

One day during a marathon meeting on contingency planning; the activity outside the conference room caught my attention and appeared more interesting than the topic being discussed inside the room. I had to be daydreaming because my attention was definitely not on the meeting. That is until someone asked, *"Paul, what do you think?"* Like a fish on a hook being snatched out of the water, my attention was yanked back into the room. I had been dreaming so long that I didn't even know the topic of discussion. I sat there with a doe-in-the-headlights look on my face trying to look intelligent and didn't utter a word. *(Better to keep your mouth shut and let them think you're a fool, than to open your mouth and eliminate all doubt!)*

Just when the silence was about to reach the moment of discomfort, Steven said, *"He doesn't know; how would he know that?"* Steven was a up–and-coming officer on-the-rise. Ivy League educated, well-respected, he was an opinion leader. Even though he let me off the hook, he did it in a way to demean not protect me.

I was humbled and humiliated. Multiple thoughts ran through my head, *"This could become my trainee legacy!"* I didn't want to be the subject of a *What-not-to-do* example passed on to future generations of trainees. *"If this goes viral I could end up working in a drive through window..."* I sat up in my chair, folded my hands and kept my eyes glued on the speaker. *(I had no desire to see the expression on anyone's face)*

The embarrassment must have heightened my ability to focus because I was in tune with everything being discussed. The contingency plan started to make sense! The meeting went on for another 30 minutes and at the conclusion the facilitator said, *"If anyone hears anything about Phil's vacation property, please let me know."*

I knew the answer, Phil told me about the vacation house he purchased that evening at the Press Club. I raised my hand and said, *"He purchased a home in Coral Gables, Florida.*" These were the first words I spoke during that 2 hour meeting.

Heads turned with smiles and amazement on the faces. Then Steven blurted out, *"Why didn't you say that when we asked you earlier?"* His smile let me know I dodged a bullet. If anyone told the Paul Bryant doe-in-the-headlights story, it had to end with Paul stealing home to win the game in the bottom of the ninth inning… Their question wasn't related to contingency planning; somebody wanted to know the depth of my relationship with Phil.

That experience taught me the importance of staying in the moment. By directing my energy toward the speaker, even though the topic was not of my liking, I was able to focus on the subject and decipher the information. I noticed that most executives used those same techniques during meetings. I labeled the actions of that process, Board Room Etiquette. (B.R.E.) For me it was standard protocol for being in a boardroom. I began to use B.R.E. in every meeting and it worked every time.

BRE is how one should physically conduct themselves in a board room or a class room. It will enable you to glean as much information as possible. When I began to lose interest in meetings I unknowingly would slouch in my chair, doodle on note pads and allow my mind to wander. B.R.E enabled me to combat a low attention span and it strengthened my ability to focus.

There are four steps to Board Room Etiquette:

1. **Both feet are flat on the floor –**
    a. Legs are not crossed and your feet are not resting on their heels.

2. **Butt is in the back of the seat –**
    a. Your Gluteus Maximus is all the way to the back of your chair. This will cause you to sit straight up in your seat. Your feet will have no other option than to sit flat on the floor and you will project great posture.

3. **Hands folded on the table unless you are taking notes –**
    a. Not only does this give the presenter the impression they have your undivided attention, it also helps you stay focused. Fiddling with pens, doodling and texting are a distraction. Folding your hands on the table will keep your mind focused on the message.

4. **Listen with your Eyes and your Ears –**
    a. Communication is an ongoing process. From the sender to the receiver and back to the sender… Maintaining visual as well as audio attention improves communication and allows the teacher or presenter to know when their message hits its mark. Looking at anything other than the speaker is interpreted by the speaker as disrespect.

       Think about it, both visual and audio senses are used to watch a television and only audio senses are used to listen to a radio. Of these two forms of media, television is able to charge much more for advertisements. Why?

Step 5:
P.L.C.

Public Speaking can be an extremely stressful experience. Some studies say it's the #1 fear of Americans. Starting and sustaining a conversation with a stranger can be equally intimidating; especially when the unfamiliar person is a senior level executive within your organization. Initiating a dialogue requires a keen level of skill and discernment. The ability to direct a conversation is an absolute must if you plan to climb the corporate ladder.

Workplace discussions are like mine fields; what's appropriate to say and what's not; how much personal information should you share and how much should you keep to yourself? The incorrect choice can blow up in your face because once words leave your mouth they can never be repealed.

Your advancement depends on knowing the difference between what's suitable and unsuitable to discuss. What do you think would be the outcome of this hypothetical situation? You are having a conversation with the president of a company you recently joined. This is your first conversation with him and it takes place at a social company event. There are a number of people standing in earshot of your discussion waiting for you to finish, so they can speak with the man. You've introduced yourself; told him what you do and what area of the organization you work. He's impressed and seems genuinely interested in getting to know you. As he starts to inquire about you, others tune in because you're new with the firm; no one really knows you and they are curious.

You perceive this is an open window of opportunity and decide to get to know him on a personal level and ask, *"So tell me, how's the wife and kids?"* What you didn't know is that he is going through an extremely bitter and public separation with his wife who owns 51% of the company. It is rumored that she will oust him as soon as the divorce is finalized. Their only child committed suicide three months earlier as a result of his infidelity and that is the reason for his impending divorce.

There are many scenarios for how this conversation might play out. Unfortunately for you, none of them are very good… But, let's say he handles the situation with diplomacy and you are able to move on with only the slightest amount of uneasiness. Every time you're in his presence you will wonder if your blunder will be held as a strike against you.

I've observed leadership on many levels and can say without reservation, the ability to communicate is an effective tool utilized in both professional and social settings. Translating thoughts into words while simultaneously making others feel important is an art that will give the possessor a strategic advantage.

I used to be intimidated by the thought of starting a conversation with a stranger. That's why I didn't engage with the other trainees on my first day of work. *"What would I say, would they be interested, would they bring up subjects I was unfamiliar with?"* I had a fear of appearing unintelligent after speaking. "*Even a fool is considered wise when he holds his peace.*" Conversations with strangers made me uncomfortable. I was a social pariah, with nothing to say. However I knew being a recluse did nothing to advance my career.

I observed people who thrived in public situations; the ones who directed the dialogue and always seemed in control. They intentionally reached out to others and involved everyone in conversations. They were the center of attention when they spoke. The more time I spent with bank executives I began to notice a pattern; a flow of inquiry that consistently led to meaningful interactions.

I labeled those topics and arranged them into a matrix called the Purpose Living Conversation or PLC. I started using PLC on the executives at the Press Club. It was an extremely effective tool that prohibited conversations from deteriorating into moments of uncomfortable silence. With PLC I directed the focus of dialogues and never had a loss for discussion topics or words. Over time, I became more comfortable in social settings and even became recognized as a good conversationalist.

PLC enables the user to start and sustain conversations; regardless of whether that conversation is with the President of their company or the President of the United States; I've tried it with both... The topics in PLC are a conversational stair step that enables the user to identify personal areas of interest that engage the responder. Pushing hot buttons is a natural progression to relationship building.

Later in my career I joined the board of an organization named, Leadership for Life. And one of the board members, Dick Amundson, introduced a teaching technique he called "the conversational stack." His 'Stack' had the same elements of PLC, but he had a unique memorization procedure that made it easy to teach. I've utilized Dick's teaching method with hundreds of students and it always works.

These are the seven topics that make the PLC matrix:

1. **Name**

   A person's name is the perfect entry point for a great conversation. People own 100% of their name; it is the sweetest sound in the world to them. When approaching a stranger you should introduce yourself first, and then ask for their name. You cannot go wrong when you start with the name.

2. **Where do you live/ originate from**

   A natural transition after learning someone's name is to find out where they live or where they are from. We all have a place of origin; a place where we reside. It's best to start on the Macro level *(Are you originally from this state/city?)* and gradually move to Micro *(What neighborhood do you live?)* as the relationship increases and everyone becomes more comfortable. On the Micro level focus on the neighborhood and not their specific home address unless arranging a visit. It's possible to hold an entire conversation on this level. (Example: You discover you are from the same city in another state, or you have family/friends that live in their hometown.) Both these scenarios are capable of taking off on their own. At the conclusion of your conversation you will have discovered common ground. And Common ground is the soil in which the seeds of a relationship begin to germinate.

3. **Family/friends**

   The next level is family and friends. Everyone has a family and most people are more than willing to discuss their family. Especially if they perceive the person making the inquiry has a genuine and sincere interest. In most situations trust will be established by your interest in their name and domicile. However, you must be astute when probing in this area and be willing to retreat at the slightest sign of trepidation. I find it best to ask open ended questions to see where the other person is willing to go. *(So, tell me about your family?)*

4. Work/School

This is a perennial favorite for most people; it's the first question they ask after learning your name. *(So, where do you work? What do you do? What school do you attend? What is your major?)* These are not bad questions; however they can pose a potential stumbling block to building a relationship.

If you ask too quickly people may perceive you are more interested in what they do rather than who they are. I've found it is always beneficial to engage them personally before going into employment/career exploration.

5. Travel

Where have you been? Where would you like to go? What have you experienced? These open ended questions allow the other person to reflect and share personal experiences. Most often they will share positive memorable moments from their past, which puts them in an optimistic frame of mind. This also allows you to gain a more intimate understanding of what they like.

6. Hobbies

Once you discover where they have been or where they would like to go, the next step is to find out what they will do when they get there. Everyone has hobbies and interest.

- i. *"Do you play tennis, golf, basketball, checkers, chess, cards – "what's your favorite game,"*
- ii. *"Do you jog, swim, watch television – "what's your favorite program,"*
- iii. *"Do you read – "what's your favorite book,"*
- iv. *Do you exercise, ride bicycles, work out, cook, fish, hunt, paint, play computer games –*
- v. *"What's your favorite," etc.*

The list is long; people enjoy talking about their interest. If you are able to uncover their hot buttons, they will do most of the talking. At the end of the night they will think you were the most engaging conversationalist they ever met.

7. **Ideas**

If you reach the idea realm of the matrix, the seeds of a relationship have started to germinate. In order for this to occur the conversation must evolve naturally.

The idea realm is not an area you can rush to achieve. If you attempt to glean someone's inner most thoughts too early or if you start sharing yours prematurely, it could have adverse effects. The other person could perceive you as prying; sticking your nose too deep in their business or TMI – giving them Too Much Information about yourself.

To do this successfully, you must become an active listener. The other person will give you permission to probe by their openness and receptivity to your conversation. You can only discover this by moving through the initial stages of PLC.

Again, it is not a race; you must allow the conversation to progress at its own pace. You might have multiple conversations with someone and not reach the idea level. Don't worry, I have known people for years and have yet to reach the idea realm. Just as water will seek its own level, your relationships will naturally find their plateau.

Remember everyone likes to feel important. If a conversation with you makes someone feel significant they will enjoy the experience and will have positive feelings toward you. Never spend too much time talking about yourself because people are more interested in their concerns than they are in yours. Find issues that are of interest to them, discuss those topics and you will be perceived as a great communicator.

Mental Preparation

It helps to have a positive mental mindset before entering into a conversation. I developed a pre-dialogue checklist to prepare for major meetings like job interviews, sales calls and presentations. I created the Mental Preparation Pyramid (MPP) and use it like the locker room pep talk delivered by the coach before the big game. MPP positions one for success in the game of life.

There are five levels in the MPP; Emotion, Action, Intent, Interest and Discovery. Like Maslow's hierarchy of needs, each region needs to be attained before you are ready to move to the next level. The first level is Emotional; it focuses on how you feel. Are you comfortable, relaxed and confident? Your emotional state plays a major role in how you are perceived and received by others. The more positive your emotional state, the more solid the foundation you have for creating a positive interaction.

This is also important for those who have leadership responsibility. Remember when you were a child in elementary school and you were called into the principal's office? There was an ominous cloud surrounding the principal's office; if you were in there, you were in trouble. Very few children were comfortable or openly shared their thoughts. Many bosses don't realize that their office may be an uncomfortable emotional meeting spot for their employees. Any leader who desires an open exchange should invest the effort to find out if their office is intimidating; if they find out that it is, they should select a meeting location that places everyone at ease.

The next level is Action. Once you have a positive Emotional state of mind, the next step is to be proactive. Do not wait on anyone to speak first; don't wait on them to select the topic of conversation. Take the initiate and show your willingness to connect. Take 100% of the responsibility and 90% of the time your effort will be reciprocated.

The third level is Intent. When you decide to take action, have a purpose. Please don't talk about abstract topics off the top of your head. This is called, *"opening your mouth and inserting your foot."* There should be an objective behind your actions; know the reason for engaging and what would be the best possible outcome.

The fourth level is Interest. You must be attentive to the person with whom you are speaking. This makes them feel significant, important and interesting. Can you think of anyone who would not like to feel significant, important or interesting? If you have ever held a conversation with someone who continually scanned the room while you were talking and in mid-sentence said, *"excuse me,"* to go speak with someone else, then you understand the negative impact of communicating with a disinterested person. It is highly unlikely you would hire that person if they showed up for an interview with you the next morning.

Discovery is the pinnacle of the Mental Preparation Pyramid. On the top level you will uncover the treasure of Common Ground, the connection points that will bring you closer. Common Ground is the fertile soil in which the seeds of a relationship are able to germinate. If nourished properly your relationships will grow into friendships.

Having friendships in the workplace is a major factor in employee satisfaction. We all have best friends, those people we like to spend our weekends with; the ones whose company we seek when we celebrate accomplishments. How much more engaged in your work could you become if your best friend was working with you on the same team trying to accomplish the same goal? Your ability to start conversations and engage others is the first step in developing and nurturing friendships.

Step 6:
Cracking the (dress) Code

YOUR DECORUM MUST RISE TO THE DIGNITY OF THE OCCASION

Most corporate leaders stand out because they dress with confidence which increases their influence. Clothes carry symbolic meanings, for example, an expensive suit indicates power, the robe of a judge implies justice and a white lab coat suggests a scientific focus.

At some point we all agonize over what's appropriate to wear. The decisions we make are important because our appearance is a determining factor in hiring and promotional decisions. Your wardrobe will not get you a promotion, but it can be a major factor holding you back. The person who is polished and sophisticated looks successful therefore, is treated as such. Employers size up applicants based on how they look and carry themselves. The clothes you wear have as much to do with first impressions as anything else. How you look can be a competitive advantage over your competition.

You begin establishing credibility in the first meeting with your manager, supervisor and co-workers. Regardless of your level of skill or the depth of your expertise, it's difficult to overcome a negative first impression. People make decisions about you five seconds after you meet. What you wear speaks volumes about your attitude toward your job, your colleagues, and yourself. Do your clothes say *'I'm promotable'* or do they say, *'I don't fit in'* or *'I don't care'?*

These are informal times; it is acceptable to wear athletic shoes to church and T Shirts to Black Tie events. However, it is still important to look professional in corporate America. Dressing appropriately shows people you are serious and understand the importance of the workplace. Proper attire greatly affects how people will treat you. According to the book, Dress for Success, "*People who look successful and well educated receive preferential treatment in almost all of their social and business encounters. Successful dress cannot put a boob in the board room, but incorrect dress can definitely keep an intelligent, able man out.*"

Not only do clothes influence the opinions of others, they also affect the way we think and feel about ourselves. We feel better when we wear clothes we like.

To some all this attention to appearance is excessive; they feel dress codes shouldn't matter. They believe the only thing that should matter is getting the job done on time with acceptable results. Well, they are wrong, your appearance does matter! Your dress might very well be the difference between success and failure. Set high expectations and your co-workers will treat you according to your professionalism. There is a place for casual attire; however it isn't the boardrooms of corporate America.

People don't follow you because they like you. They follow because they respect you. People who look successful are more likely to get positive results—whether it's being seated at a "good table" in a restaurant or persuading superiors that they are the right person for the promotion. The Harvard Business Review notes that 37 percent of men believe that if you don't look the part of a leader, you're not going to get a leadership role yourself.

Your clothes produce four beneficial workplace attributes that will help you move up the corporate ladder:

1. Acceptance
2. Respect
3. Credibility
4. Authority

Obtain these four qualities and your upward mobility will be much greater than someone who lacks them. Make them a part of your brand and they will be assets for you when dealing with others.

The following tips will help you avoid sartorial landmines in the workplace. Some of them you may already know. I learned many of them as a child sitting at the dinner table. However, when dealing with something as important as your career it is never a bad idea to take a review.

Dress for the position you want, not the one you have. This may mean dressing more formally than your peers, but if you have the option, it's to your advantage to dress prosperously. Your success may hinge on your ability to select clothing, jewelry and hairstyles that enhance your professional image.

Never wear sunglasses in the office and avoid glasses that change tint as the light changes. People must see your eyes to develop trust in you; remember the importance of eye contact. Make sure your hair is clean, neat and professionally styled. Your attire must always be clean, neatly pressed and should fit well.

Darker colors like black, navy and gray give an authoritative message. They influence others and give the impression you know what you are doing. Lighter colors like pastels and yellow are less intimidating. People may associate someone who wears them as being kind, welcoming, and friendly.

Red universally means stop, danger or excitement. Wear this color when you want to attract attention. Blue on the other hand, is relaxing. Blue may be the color to wear during an interview or for that big promotion.

Rules for women:

Make sure your clothes aren't too tight. Close-fitting clothes may attract attention, but trust me; it's not the type of attention that will gain respect or sustain your career in the long run. Select clothes that draw the eye to your face. Wear skirts that are long enough and loose enough for you to sit, stand, pick up your purse and not show your thighs. Always wear neutral, non-patterned nylons/pantyhose/tights—no bare legs. If you must wear color, choose colors that coordinate with your skirt and carry an extra pair in case of runs. Avoid wearing clothes that are too trendy. You don't want your outfit to stand out more than you do.

Select blouses that provide visual interest, but no cleavage. You want people to be thinking about how competent you are, so avoid clothes that are transparent, have low necklines, revealing waistlines or detract from your face as a focal point. And never wear cocktail attire to the office.

Wear flat shoes or low pumps in colors that avoid making your feet a focal point, typically in black or brown. Be sure that they are clean and polished and avoid open-toed shoes. I know Flat shoes and low heels are not the latest fashion trend and many women prefer higher heels. The most important thing is to look professional with the ability to move easily. The last thing you want is a pair of shoes that hurt your feet.

Your makeup, nail polish, perfume, jewelry and hair should be low-key and non-distracting. Avoid large dangling earrings and wear no more than a simple necklace, one ring per hand and a nice watch. Make sure your hair does not fall in your face or cover your eyes and if you have facial piercings, remove them. These tips will ensure your wardrobe selection is never the topic of conversation around the water coolers at your office.

Rules for men:

The last thing anyone wants to make is an office faux-pas, so let's first define casual wear for the office. Office casual does not mean the comfy clothes you wear when you kick it on the weekends. In corporate culture casual attire means a shirt with a collar, slacks or khakis. The shoes of choice are Dockers or some type of loafer, never sandals or Jordan's.

Standard corporate attire is a black, dark blue, gray or charcoal suit. The darker the suit, the more authority it transmits. The most authoritative pattern is the pinstripe, followed by the solid, the chalk stripe and the plaid.

Your shirt should be white or light-colored and long sleeved. It should always look pressed; you never want to look wrinkled. Make certain your shirt fits around the neck and your wrist. A common mistake many entry level employees make is wearing shirts that are the wrong size. If you don't know your shirt size, go to a store with a men's clothing department and ask them to measure you. The dimensions you receive will be for the size of your neck and the length of your sleeves. 17/35 means you have a 17 inch neck and length of your sleeves is 35 inches.

If your pants have belt loops, wear a belt that coordinates with your shoes. And please, never make the unforgivable mistake of wearing a belt and suspenders together.

The tie is your area for self-expression. Choose a silk tie and make sure it contrasts with the color of your shirt. Be careful in your choice of patterns. A Mickey Mouse tie might be acceptable if you are working for the Disney Corporation but it might not fly at Bank of America. When in doubt, be conservative.

Your Shoes should be conservative, clean, and polished. Buy a pair of leather shoes, something plain and comfortable. Black shoes go well with black, navy or gray. Brown shoes go well with khaki or brown. Select leather belts that visually blend or match your shoes and wear dark socks that match — never, ever wear white socks with a suit!

Athletic shoes have elevated in stature. They have become acceptable attire in many venues; however, corporate America is not one of them! It doesn't matter what the celebrities are wearing, leave your running shoes at the gym.

Avoid necklaces, body piercings and earrings. Wear no more than one ring per hand. In fact, minimize all jewelry! Make sure your hair is neat, your moustache and beard are well groomed, your fingernails are clean and your cologne should never be strong.

Step 7:
Time Principal

TO BE EARLY IS TO BE ON TIME.
TO BE ON TIME IS TO BE LATE.
AND TO BE LATE,
IS TO SOON BE FORGOTTEN!

GALE SAYERS

Former NFL running back, Gale Sayers, is notorious for showing up ½ hour early to meetings. This made life particularly challenging for me as the coordinator of the Gale Sayers Golf Classic. He would always arrive early and expect everyone else to do the same. I jumped through a few hurdles before I learned how to manage his working style and he developed trust in mine.

One morning I scheduled a press conference at my office for 8:00am. Gale arrived at 7:30am and I arrived at 7:35am. He didn't like waiting in front of an empty building and he was concerned as to why there were no reporters. He wanted to know if I had properly notified the press and if so, were they planning to attend. As the minutes ticked away, he started to inquire about other details of the tournament; it appeared he was unsure if I was on top of the details. This created a delicate situation as I had to direct my staff as they arrived (late in Gale's eyes) while the tournament host was looking over my shoulder. Once the press arrived Gale's concerns were eliminated. However, I made a mental note to always arrive 45 minutes early when dealing with Gale Sayers.

Why am I talking about a sports figure when this book is about navigating corporate culture? Well, quite frankly Gale Sayers is unique; he is not the stereotypical professional athlete. Yes, he is he the youngest person admitted into the NFL Hall of Fame. Yes, he is one of the top running backs of all time who burst onto the NFL scene by setting the record for touchdowns in a season with 22 and winning Rookie of the Year honors. Yes, he broke the record for the most touchdowns in a game with six, a record that still stands. And yes, he was selected as an All Pro in his first five seasons and is still regarded as the greatest return man to ever play the game with an unreal 30.56 yard average; an NFL record that stands to this day.

Yes, he is also the author of two books, 'I am Third' and 'The life and Times of Gale Sayers'. And yes, the Emmy Award winning movie, Brian's Song, details his relationship with fellow teammate, Brian Piccolo, when they became the first black and white roommates in the NFL.

What I find striking is that of all the information available on Gale Sayers, the most under published are the details of his success as a businessman. He is the founder and Chairman of the Sayers Group LLC. His company has offices in five cities with

$300 million in annual revenues. Gale Sayers is not the typical athlete.

In 1970, I had the pleasure of meeting Mr. Sayers. That meeting left an indelible impression on me as a thirteen year old kid. From that moment forward I had visions of greatness. I followed Gale's accomplishments the same as I followed Phil's at the bank. When I had the honor of meeting him as an adult and convinced him to allow me to create a tournament bearing his name, I took every opportunity to learn from him.

He is a guy from my hometown who reached the pinnacle of success in many different arenas. So if the great Gale Sayers says to be early is to be on time… Who am I not to listen?

It is always best to get to meetings early. This gives you an opportunity to get settled, make necessary preparations or adjustments and if you need to, extinguish any 11th hour brush fires.

Step 8:
P^5

PROPER **P**LANNING **P**REVENTS **P**OOR **P**ERFORMANCE
OR
PRESENTING YOURSELF **P**ROPERLY REQUIRES **P**LANNING, **P**REPARATION AND **P**URPOSE

His first comment after reviewing the outline for this book was, "*Make sure you don't exclude Purpose. It's important for everyone in business to know their purpose.*" I thought this was very intuitive because my first book, *The **Purpose Living Leader***, centered on identifying your individual talents and focusing on your reasons for existence. The most happy and engaged people in life know their purpose and actively use their abilities to attain worthy goals and ideas. Without purpose life is just an experiment.

That friend, John Kotouc, is an analytical thinking obsessive learner. He is an alum of Harvard University who always drills deeper searching for truth. He challenges me to be better and has supported my political campaigns, non-profit missions and entrepreneurial endeavors. Besides being a great person, a confidant, and someone in my corner, John is also the Chairman of the American National Bank. His bank is the metro's second largest privately-held bank with over 2 Billion in Assets.

It's quite affirming to know that someone on his level; a high achiever according to the worldly standards, believes purpose is an important trait.

I dedicate this chapter to **John Kotouc.** Someone who knows that true success is having joy in your heart, purpose in your step and passion for what you do… John believes leadership is for life and a leaders Influence should Inspire Integrity in others.

This chapter is ripe with the do's and don'ts to help people stay on purpose. Because it's easy to lose focus while clamoring to succeed, especially once you've acquired several of your bucket-list goals.

Success or failure in corporate America may depend on your ability to understand the importance of every personal encounter. You've heard it before; **p**roper **p**lanning **p**revents **p**oor **p**erformance. Every time you are in the presence of superiors you should maximize the moment. P^5 is a sure fire way to avoid making missteps, it is an important acronym to remember as you climb the ladder to success.

Every time you have the opportunity to shine, take it! I'm not suggesting you become the proverbial suck-up; nobody likes that. What I mean however, is that on those days when your shine has dwindled to a twinkle, avoid interaction, if you can.

For example, never schedule a meeting with your boss just to dump your personal problems on his desk, while discussing nothing work related. He may listen and even offer great advice, but too many of these meetings will cause him to see you as not being able to handle your personal life. He may not envision you as a fit for advancement because you have too many personal problems and you haven't demonstrated the ability to reconcile them with your work.

Never show up to the staff meetings sneezing and blowing your nose with a 102 degree temperature. You won't get points for being a trooper. Showing up sick will annoy your co-workers for exposing them to your germs and jeopardizing their health.

Preparation is always being ready to seize the moment. This is the logic behind having an elevator speech. At any moment you should be prepared to deliver your position on an issue within the time it takes to complete a normal elevator ride from the top to the bottom floor. Your mission is to get your point across in a timely manner; to start a conversation and convince them you are somebody worth knowing.

An elevator speech is a great tool to use with busy executives. The following story is an example of how preparation and planning helped advance my career. I came to work early one morning and the only other passenger on the elevator was an older gentleman. I said, *"Good Morning"* and he returned my greeting. I made a general comment about the weather and it being a great day to work at the bank. He asked my name and inquired as to why I was so early. I replied, *"My name is Paul Bryant, I'm a Management trainee. I'm early because the early bird catches the worm."* He smiled and gave a witty response, *"he also gets the best parking space."* We both chuckled, the door opened, passengers boarded and our conversation ended. The elevator reached the executive floor and the older gentleman stepped off. As he passed he said to me, *"Go get that worm."* I responded. "*Yeah, you already have the parking spot."* As soon as the door closed a murmur erupted among the other passengers. *"Was that Phil? I think so; I've never seen him before. I've been working here 10 years and I haven't met him. Who? That old guy was Phil?"*

I asked, *"Who is Phil?"* To my surprise, I had unknowing joked around with the former President of the bank! Judging from the reactions from the other people on the elevator Phil was unapproachable. It seemed odd to me that people were in awe of the kind gentleman I had just met. I couldn't wait to tell the other trainees about my experience and found that neither of them had met him nor knew what he looked like.

I decided Phil was someone I wanted to know better. I needed a plan; I couldn't just walk in his office and say, *"Hi! My name is Paul and I'd like to be friends."* So I developed a strategy to reengage with him and provide introductions for my fellow trainees.

I asked my classmates if they would like to meet him because I planned to ask Phil for a meeting. *"As future leaders of the bank, we should have relationships with executives at the highest levels in the organization."* They doubted I would do it, so I called Phil right there on the spot. I fully expected an administrative assistant to answer the phone, but he answered. With no time to waffle I said, *"This is Paul Bryant, the trainee you met on the elevator this morning. I was sharing with my classmates that I met you and found that none of my colleagues has met you. We have the pleasure of meeting with executives in all areas of the bank and I was wondering if you wouldn't mind meeting with us?"* He said, *"I'd be delighted to meet with your associates. In fact, I'll do you one better, Paul do you think they would mind having lunch with me?"* Of course we accepted his offer and we became the first trainee class to have a private luncheon on the terrace level of the bank.

Once I found out who Phil was, I developed a plan to get to know him. By sharing the opportunity with my classmates it became a win-win-win situation. It's an added plus to advance your cause and do something good for others in the process.

I had two opportunities with Phil; first, on the elevator and again on the telephone. The way I presented myself shaped his impression of me. The only way to make that happen was to implement a plan that would allow me to engage with him. **P**resenting myself **P**roperly required **P**lanning and **P**reparation with a **P**urpose, however, P^5 is much more than an elevator speech.

When speaking with individuals at higher levels within your company you need to know as much about the business as possible; not only what the products and services are, but company history; where did the organization start, do they have other locations, are they a parent or subsidiary company, who is the competition, what is their strategic advantage, what is the mission statement and what are the future plans of the company. These are the topics you will want to be conversant on when interacting vertically.

You also want to find out as much information about individual leaders of your company as you can. With linkedIn, Facebook, Google and the company website you can find information on just about anyone. You want to know the organizational chart, how many levels you need to climb to reach your goal, where leaders previously worked, where they attended college, what cities, states, countries they previously lived, what clubs/ organizations/ fraternities/ sororities they belong to, are they married, do they have kids, how long they have been with the company and what was their path of progression.

The answers to these questions will equip you to engage them in a conversation that goes deeper than the surface. Remember the lessons from P.L.C.:

- Everyone likes to feel important.
- Find issues that are of interest to them, discuss those topics and you will be perceived as a great communicator.
- If conversations with you make people feel significant they will enjoy the experience and will have positive feelings toward you.

You must be proactive and ask for opportunities. Career changing events are made; they don't just fall at your feet. Ask your boss if you can take something off his plate, he will love your initiative. The greater the risk you take, the greater the reward.

When I was in college, becoming a Vice President was one of my career goals. The following story details how I took on an assignment that resulted in my promotion to Vice President and Division Manager for The Gallup International Division of Public Safety.

I had only been employed with the company for 5 months. I was the National Director of Marketing in the Associations Division, the most profitable unit of the company. I reported directly to the Division Manager, a senior vice President who was extremely successful. He was a multi-year recipient of the sales leadership award and had one of the highest salaries in the company. He was a hard charger who achieved considerable success; however he treated his team like indentured servants.

It wasn't uncommon for him to publicly dress down a staff member; no one was exempt, he treated us like inferior beings. I once watched him make a grown man cry.

Even though I had only been with the company for 5 months that was long enough to assess his management style and the culture of his department. I didn't like it, but the money was great. I tried to prepare myself for my inevitable turn on the hot seat, but there is no adequate preparation for willful and intentional humiliation.

He made a comment that was out of line and cut deep. I told him, *"I respect you and I demand that you respect me! I will not be talked to like a child."* His immediate response was, *"Why don't we just make this your two week notice..."* The mere fact that I had the courage to stand my ground was a terminable offense in his eyes.

I walked out of his office directly to the office of the President. I asked for a minute of his time and immediately shared with him my version of the story. He asked if there was any way things could be reconciled. I said, *"No. it really isn't a good fit, so I will only be with the company for two more weeks."* He asked if there was anything else I could do for the company and I responded, *"Yeah, I can do his job!"*

His look intensified and he asked if I knew anything about law enforcement because the company was considering creating a division that focused on Public Safety. They were currently assessing the opportunities and were gathering as much information as possible. He was headed to Washington D.C. in two days and asked if I could schedule some meetings for him with opinion leaders in the law enforcement field.

I jumped at the opportunity and returned to his office three hours later with meetings scheduled with the Executive Director of the International Association of Chiefs of Police, the Executive Director of the Police Executive Research Forum and the director of the Police Policy Board for the U.S, Conference of Mayors.

He was amazed at the level of individuals I was able to contact and the promptness of my response. He invited me to attend the meetings with him and they all went well. On the flight home he turned to me and said, *"You will lead this new division for us. You're a Vice President now, get some new business cards made."*

Sometimes it's necessary to take risks. Ask to work on projects that operate at the level you aspire to reach. This gives superiors and opportunity to see your work first hand. A year later I was promoted to Senior Vice President and created the Division of Urban Affairs.

Because I was able to **P**resent myself **P**roperly with a **P**lan, I became the first African American Vice President in the history of The Gallup Organization.

Step 9:
BOARDroom GAMES

IT'S LIKE PLAYING A GAME OF CHESS ON A MONOPOLY BOARD.
YOU'RE PLAYING A GREAT GAME, BUT YOU WILL NEVER WIN,
BECAUSE YOU ARE PLAYING BY THE WRONG RULES.

Learn to play BOARD room games. The most common in corporate America are golf, tennis and bridge. These games provide out-of-the-office interactions which are really where relationships are built. You don't want to be the person who stays back at the office on Friday's because everyone else is participating in the golf league.

It's also important to learn the culture of your particular organization, because every company has its own distinct values. Example: It's a common fact that President Obama is an avid basketball player. He enjoys the sport so much he had a basketball court built in the White House. I've heard that select staffers frequently participate in competitive games. I'd bet my life savings that a white house intern who was a college basketball star would have the opportunity to interface with the President.

I once worked in Washington D.C. on a grant for the International Association for Chiefs of Police (IACP). Every Saturday I played football with a select group lead by the Secretary of Education, Bill Bennett. Bill had visions of being a great quarterback. Most of the players were members of his staff. Bill always played quarterback and I was always his first pick.

I was the deep ball threat; it made his day to throw the ball as far and as high as he could and for me to run under it and make the catch for a touchdown. It was kind of cool; the guy giving me a high five on Saturday was the same guy on Meet-the-Press on Sunday.

I was invited to participate in that group because I played football in college. Because of those Saturday games, I made several lasting relationships and now you know how I was able to arrange those meetings so quickly for the President of The Gallup Organization.

It's a common saying that deals are done on the golf course. I don't know if that is true. I think people decide if you are someone they would like to do business with on the golf course. A wide range of your emotions will show during a round of Golf. Do you get angry after a bad shot? Do you gloat when you win a hole? Do you tease or support your playing partner? A person can gain an insight into how you do business by how you conduct yourself during a round of golf. This is true with any game. Games are social, unofficial opportunities for participants to access your character and competitiveness. The final analysis is not whether or not you win the game, its weather or not they want you as a member of their team.

When interacting with executives' who are levels above you; it's important to know who you are and your reason for being there. You don't want to be a corporate groupie acting like a teenage fan with a backstage pass, enamored to simply be in the room. Have a reason, a purpose, know the issues within your company and how you add value. Then when your window of opportunity opens, you are prepared to jump through with both feet.

Unfortunately, many young employees unknowingly blow these opportunities. People who don't know what they have are destined to abuse it. An opportunity not taken is an opportunity lost. Remember, to present yourself properly you must have a plan and you should be prepared, but the essential element is having a purpose for your actions.

No matter how friendly you become, your co-workers and bosses are business relationships and should be treated accordingly. The office is not a coffee shop, it's not the community center, it isn't a lounge and it's definitely not the pick-up spot.

Respect yourself and the coworkers in your office and people will admire you.

It is extremely important for anyone looking to get ahead to have a sense of purpose in both their personal and professional lives. You need to know the reason for your actions. People who don't stand for something will fall for anything.

SUMMARY

DO THESE STEPS WORK?

You need to go no further for validation. I successfully used EVERY step in this book. They work! Learn these nine steps and you will be able to maneuver up or down any ladder you wish. From the backstreets to the boardrooms, from the streets to the suites; I've been there. I've dealt with those high in society and the least in notoriety. Successfully navigating corporate culture is an art. You are the artist, your job is the canvas and the nine steps are your paint brushes. You are ready, go forth and make a masterpiece. And remember, the ladder of success is never crowded at the top!

In the following story I used all nine steps; you judge for yourself if they were helpful. You determine if I achieved a desirable outcome.

This experience takes place in Detroit, Michigan. I was a participant in the Isaiah Thomas Celebrity Golf Tournament. My mission was to do more than shoot a low round of golf; Isaiah had recently shelled out $10 million dollars to purchase the Continental Basketball Association (CBA) and I wanted to introduce him to the consulting services of my company. Isaiah's athletic accomplishments were well known, however his track record in business was yet to be determined. I knew my company could assist him in his new capacity as league owner.

I didn't have a meeting scheduled with him; but I decided to take a calculated risk. I registered for his tournament and planned to make something happen. When the timing was right I intended to introduce myself to Isaiah and familiarize him with our management consulting practice. (**P^3**)

The round of golf ended and the awards dinner was about to begin. I was one of 300 people milling about the banquet hall waiting for the program to begin. Standing in the middle of the room was Isaiah Thomas, Julius Erving and Stedman Graham; they seemed to be engaged in an intense discussion. Everyone stood around the edges of the room discreetly watching and wondering what the 'big boys' were talking about.

For those of you who don't know, Isaiah Thomas is a two time world champion, who played for the Detroit Pistons. He is a former All Star, who is a member of the NBA Hall of Fame. Julius Erving, aka Dr. J, is also a member of the Hall of Fame and world champion who played with the Philadelphia 76rs. He is considered one of the best players to ever play the game of basketball. Stedman Graham is a motivational speaker and author often noted for his long standing relationship with Oprah Winfrey.

I stood there, on the outskirts of the room, watching and wondering with everyone else. Suddenly it hit me, NOW is the time to make something happen! (**Time Principal**) Once the banquet started we'd have to sit through the program. Then when the program ended I'd have to compete with other attendees for Isaiah's attention. The last thing I wanted was to be standing in a line, business card in hand waiting for my two minutes to make an impression *(This is a major problem with prospecting at social events)*

I had an internal conversation with my ego, *"You are a senior executive with an international corporation with valuable services to sell. You are in the same room, attending the same event; you are supposed to be here! Now is the time to make them aware of your presence.*" (**P.I.E. Theory**)

I walked over to them with a smile on my face, held my hand out and introduced myself (**SPAM & Executive Handshake**). After the introduction I said, *"Everyone in the room is wondering what you guys are discussing, it has to be your shirts.*" All three were wearing the latest edition of Nike golf shirts. These shirts had neon colors and extreme patterns that made them very distinctive. All three chuckled and one of them joked, *"Is this your way of fishing for a compliment?"* (**Dress Code**) I was wearing one also...

One of them asked what I did for a living and that was the opening I needed to start a **Purpose Living Conversation. (P.L.C.)** By the time we got around to discussing the CBA we were sitting at a table in the awards banquet and I was in full focus mode, **(B.R.E.)**

Fast forward three weeks from that meeting and I had a signed contract with the Continental Basketball Association for $800,000. Nine months later Stedman Graham included my story in his book, *Build Your Own Life Brand.* And 18 months later my wife and I received an invitation from Oprah Winfrey to attend a seven day cruise to honor the 70th birthday of Dr. Maya Angelo. This invitation was a result of the friendship I had established with Stedman.

The eight steps in this book are guaranteed to equip you with everything to build long-term mutually beneficial relationships. A journey of 1,000 miles begins with the first step. You must first build a relationship with someone before they are willing to do business with you.

So, how would I handle my first day as a management trainee knowing what I know today?

The first thing I would do differently is change the wardrobe selection. I'd wear a dark blue suit with a starched white shirt. The tie would be silk and some shade of light blue. The color choices would be strategic; on the first day I would present a calming presence of authority. My goal would be to make as many friends as I could.

My day would start 20 minutes earlier. Instead of walking through the door at 8:00am I'd arrive at 7:40. This would allow time for a cup of coffee and provide the opportunity to meet people and familiarize myself with the office before the day began. *To be early is to be on time, to be on time is to be late, And to be late is to soon be forgotten...*

Next, armed with the Executive handshake and PLC, I'd walk through the door open and receptive to interacting with every person I met. I'd be proactive, intentionally reaching out to others, not waiting to be invited. Every person I encountered would remember meeting Paul Bryant on his first day and how excited he was to be there. My enthusiasm would be contagious.

A successful first day is as simple as following the golden rule; "*Do unto others as you would have others do unto you...*" You see, people don't remember what you said, and most won't remember what you did; at the end of the day what they will remember is how you made them feel. I would intentionally uplift everyone around me which would cause them to like me.

In corporate America, everyone is looking to get ahead, that's the culture. You need to understand this is fact before stepping in the building. The key to building constituencies is to value the people you meet. Treat everyone with respect. Allow your coworkers to observe your character as well as your abilities. When they perceive you as an ally and not as opposition, you will be welcomed with open arms.

You don't have to be cut-throat to get ahead. *"A rising tide lifts all boats."* Learn to be tolerant of those who don't always agree with you, say kind words to those you don't admire and form the habit of looking for the good instead of the bad in others. Take the time to appreciate people as you ascend the corporate ladder, it will make the climb more enjoyable. Your co-workers will support you if they perceive a benefit from your achievement. *Can you think of anyone who would not like to have a relationship with the CEO of their company???*

It's not personal, it's human nature; we hire and promote the people we Know, Trust and Like.

REFERENCES

<u>**Dress for Success - Book Summary Prepared by Robert Wayne**</u>
www.grandpappy.info/bdress.htm

<u>**Ten Commandments - Computer Ethics Institute**</u>
computerethicsinstitute.org/publications/tencommandments.html

<u>**Easy Etiquette for Preteens: Minding Your Manners**</u>
www.pamf.org

<u>**The Secret of the Perfect Handshake - Body Language Expert, Patti ...**</u>
www.pattiwood.net

<u>**Soft Skills vs Hard Skills | Teachers' Letters to Bill Gates**</u>
teachersletterstobillgates.com

<u>**Issue Brief on Workforce Readiness - America's Promise Alliance**</u>
www.americaspromise.org

<u>**PDK/Gallup Poll | PDK International - Phi Delta Kappa International**</u>
pdkintl.org/programs-resources/poll/

<u>**Beyond the headlines - Seattle Jobs Initiative**</u>
www.seattlejobsinitiative.com

<u>**James J. Heckman - The University of Chicago Library**</u>
www.lib.uchicago.edu

<u>**Issue Brief on Workforce Readiness - America's Promise Alliance**</u>
www.americaspromise.org

REFERENCES

<u>Shemlah Naphish : The Emory Wheel</u>
www.emorywheel.com

<u>The Soft Skills Managers Want - Businessweek</u>
www.businessweek.com

<u>"Hard" Skills Trump "Soft" Skills - Harvard Business Review</u>
blogs.hbr.org

Paul Bryant is the Founder of the Leadership Institute for Urban Education. He teaches a Leadership course at the University of Nebraska-Omaha and holds the distinction of being the nation's most versatile educator; teaching elementary, middle, high school, college and incarcerated youth.

Paul earned two Masters Degrees from the University of Nebraska, and received a full scholarship to Creighton University law school. He served as the CEO of three different nonprofit agencies:

*The United Methodist Community Centers, Inc.
*The Urban League of Nebraska, and
*The United Minority Contractors Association

His corporate career includes a Senior Vice President post with The Gallup Organization, as well as Business Banker and Officer Positions with Wells Fargo and the First National Bank of Omaha.

In 2005 Paul left a 25 year corporate career to manage a struggling non-profit agency. This move placed him on the path toward his purpose. Today, he is a Pulitzer Prize nominated author and his leadership influence extends to more than ½ million students through an international network of over 1,500 schools.

Paul is a respected voice of leadership inspiring Educators, Corporate Executives and leaders of Religious, Public and Private institutions to live their purpose. His teaching resonates with people of all ages, races and economic backgrounds. His message is simple; ***"We are born with innate talents. The most successful people in life are those who know their strengths and utilize their gifts to attain a worthy goal or idea."***

He is the recipient of numerous awards, including: the City of Omaha's Martin Luther King "Living the Dream" Award and the University of Nebraska's Alumnus Achievement Award. He was twice selected as the Teacher of the year for the Creighton University Upward Bound program; named "Facilitator of the Year" by INROADS Inc., and named an Achiever to watch in the Millennium Success Guide. He was chosen as one of the Ten Outstanding Young Omahans by the Junior Chamber of Commerce and named a Black Achiever by the YMCA. Paul is also a member of the prestigious Benson High School Hall of Fame,

along with other noted Omahans like investor Warren Buffett. His most prized accomplishment however, is being recognized along with his family, as the 2011 Community Service Family of the year, by the Heartland Family Service.

Paul is a Christian and his mission in life is to inspire people to live their purpose. He authored two other books, The Purpose Living Leader and the I^3 Journal. The Purpose Living Leader was nominated for a Pulitzer Prize and was utilized as curriculum at Creighton University, the University of Nebraska at Omaha and Metropolitan Community College.

The Purpose Living series of work targets emotional and moral instruction. The message was originally extended to young men, but now reaches women and adults of all races and ages. The logo shows an instructor organizing a group of students with his focus on the very young and as they get older, they are further back in the line-up, more and more ready to go out on their own with the lessons learned.

Anyone looking for encouragement or validation should hear Paul speak, he doesn't just talk about success and leadership; he lives it!

To purchase books, or hire Paul for a keynote speech or training session; email him at:

liue@cox.net

Leadership Institute for Urban Education©

CPSIA information can be obtained at www.ICGtesting.com
Printed in the USA
LVOW12*0802130314

377181LV00001B/2/P

9 781600 479366